MARTIN LEMAN

COMIC & CURIOUS CATS

WORDS BY ANGELA CARTER

H·A·R·M·O·N·Y B·O·O·K·S

NEW YORK

I love my cat with an

Because he is Amiable
Amenable
Altogether Adorable
His name is Abednigo
He lives in Appletreewick
He Artfully eats Artichokes

I love my cats with a

BC

and a

Because they are Beautiful and Capricious
Beatific if Clamorous
Brisk yet Calm
Their names are Basil and Clarissa
They live in Brandon Creek
And they eat Begonias and Carnations
To my Bewildered Consternation

I love my cat with a

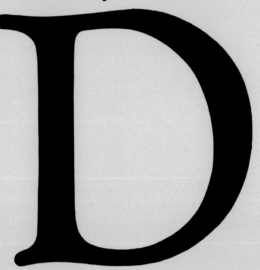

Because he is Diabolic
Dramatic
And Debonair
His name is Dominic
He lives in Diss
He Daringly eats Dragees
Devilled Drumsticks and Doughnuts
(Although he leaves the holes)

I love my cat with an

Although she is Elephantine
Epicurean
And Edacious
Her name is Emilia
She lives in Edgware
And she eats Everything Earnestly

I love my cats with an

and a

Because they are Fleet and Gracile
Flirtatious and Gourmandising
If Freakish and Garrulous
Their names are Francesca and Gordon
They live in FotherinGay
Frequently and Gladly
They eat Fried Fish and Gobstoppers
With Forks and Gloves

I love my cat with an

H

In spite of his Hypochondria
Because he is Handsome
And Humane
His name is Horatio
He lives in Hastings
He eats Herrings, Hake
And Haddock Happily

I love my cat with an

I

Because he is Ingenious
Ingenuous
And Insinuating
His name is Inigo
He lives in Inverurie
He eats Inkfish Incessantly

I love my cat with a

JKL

Because she is Joking, Kindly, Loving
Jumping, Kinetic, Light-footed
Judicious, Knowing, Lyrical
Her name is JacKieLynn
She lives in Klapham Junction, London
She eats Jellybabies
Kohlrahbi and Liquorice
Just as Quick as Lightning

I love my cats with an

MNO

Because they are Merry, Neat and Oscillating
Madcap, Necessary and Ostentatious
Moody, Notorious and Omnivorous
Their names are Mildred, Norman and Oliver
They live in Midsomer NortOn
They eat Meatpies, Nut-cutlets, Oranges
And Much else besides, Not all of it Official

I love my cat with a

P

and a Q

Because he is Provocative and Questioning
Pertinacious and Quick-sighted
Though Prone to Quest
His name is PasQuale
He moved to Puddletown from Queen Camel
He eats Partridge, Quince jelly
And Queen of Puddings
Purring Querulously

I love my cat with an

RST

Because he is Rational, Sensitive and Tractable
Regal, Serene and Tolerant
Robust, Sincere and Thoughtful
His name is Raymond Stafford-Tracey
He lives in Rooms in Stoke-on-Trent
He eats Raspberries, Strawberries
And Toad-in-the-hole
He Rarely Seems Troubled

I love my cat with a

U

Although he is Ungrateful
Ugly
And Untrustworthy
His name is Unwin
He lives in Ullapool
And eats Up all the leftovers Ungraciously

I love my cat with a

Because he is Vigorous
Versatile
Never Vindictive
His name is Vivaldi
He lives in Virkie
He eats his Vegetables
For the sake of the Vitamins

I love my cat with a

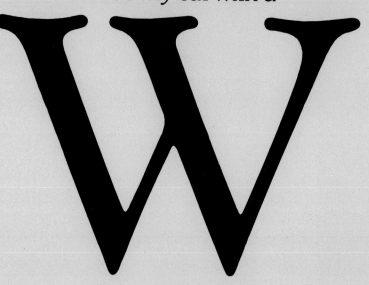

Because he is Watchful
And Wakeful
Although he sometimes Worries
His name is Wilberforce
He lives in West Wittering
He eats Watercress, Windfalls –
Whatever he can get
Wistfully Winking

I love my cat with an

XYZ

There is really nothing more to be said

Martin Leman was born in London in 1934, son of a Covent Garden fruit merchant. Most of his early memories are unhappy ones of evacuation and various boarding schools. After two years in the army, he trained and worked as a typographer. His main interest was chess until 1969, when he started painting. His first one-man exhibition was held in London in 1971, and he has subsequently exhibited throughout Great Britain and Europe. He lives and works in Islington, North London.

Angela Carter's literary career began at the age of six when she wrote and illustrated the now lost *Tom Catt Goes to Market*. She has since established a firm reputation as one of the most original and stylish talents writing today. She is the author of seven novels and two collections of short stories, and has won both the Somerset Maugham and the John Llewellyn Rhys Awards. She lives in London.

Printed in Italy by A. Mondadori Editore, Verona
Designed by Philippa Bramson

ISBN 0-517-537532